TOP SECRET

Survival
GUIDE

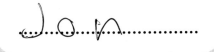

Access
restricted
to: ▶▶▶▶▶ ....J..o..n..............

Secrets of Survival

Be prepared to survive anything, from **CHARGING ELEPHANTS** to a car journey **YAWN-A-THON**, with your own totally **Top Secret Survival Guide.** First take the quiz, then discover the secrets of **OUTDOOR** and **EXTREME** survival, and finally devise your own **SECRET PLANS!**

WOULD YOU SURVIVE?

Take this test to find out, and then check the answers on page 6.

1

How can you tell the difference between a crocodile and an alligator?

a. Their snouts are a different shape.

b. Their tails are a different length.

c. Their feet are a different size.

2

Can you identify the ridge tent?

a.

b.

c.

3

Clouds can help you . . .

a. tell the time

b. forecast the weather

c. figure out your direction of travel

4

Which of these can be a source of water in an emergency?

a. plants

b. fallen leaves

c. tree bark

5

What is the international signal for help?

a. SAS

b. SIS

c. SOS

6

Which of these should you NEVER do?

a. make eye contact with a bear

b. hide your food from a bear

c. back away slowly from a bear

9

Sunglasses protect your eyes from which rays?

a. stingrays

b. IV rays

c. UV rays

10

Which of these is not a type of knot?

a. bowline

b. bovine

c. clove hitch

7

What is a cipher?

a. a gadget to purify water

b. a form of secret message writing

c. a type of snake

11

In freezing conditions, if you don't wear a hat, how much of your body heat can be lost through your head?

a. up to 100%

b. up to 40%

c. up to 10%

8

How fast can lava flow?

a. 5 mph (8 km/h)

b. 20 mph (32 km/h)

c. 40 mph (65 km/h)

12

In which direction does the sun set?

a. west

b. north

c. south

WOULD YOU SURVIVE?

ANSWERS

1. a
2. b
3. b
4. a
5. c
6. a
7. b
8. c
9. c
10. b
11. b
12. a

HOW DID YOU SCORE?

11–12
Awesome! You are prepared for almost any survival scenario.

6–10
You have a great basic knowledge, but there is always more to discover.

1–5
Your survival knowledge is limited, but you are in the right place to learn more.

Secrets of Outdoor Survival

BASIC EQUIPMENT

Surviving the great outdoors requires smarts, stamina, and the right equipment. Here are some essentials.

BACKPACK

A waterproof backpack is essential for keeping your equipment safe. Make sure it has lots of pockets and is not too heavy. Pack the things you'll need last at the bottom of the bag and keep items like snacks and a medical kit in the easy-to-reach side pockets.

MAP

contour lines

Even if you have GPS on your phone, you should have a **paper map** – you never know when you might lose your signal. Before you set off, study the map:

Check the **scale** of the map and practice measuring the distance between key areas.

Find out where there are **lakes and rivers** for water, and **forests** for shelter.

Check the **contour lines**. If they are close together, the area will have steep slopes.

Research your location to find out what else you might need.

SOS! :-O

CELL PHONE

A phone is an important tool, but unless you have a solar charger, keep it for **emergency use only** – so no music and no games!

SUNGLASSES AND SUNSCREEN

You will need both of these to protect your eyes and skin from UV rays.

PENS AND PAPER

You may want to **record your journey**, leave messages along the way, or draw maps, so make sure you have two pens (one as a spare) and a lightweight pad of paper.

FLASHLIGHT

A wind-up flashlight is best as it does not need batteries. Make sure it has a bright light so you can draw attention to yourself in an emergency.

FIRST-AID KIT

What you need in your kit will depend on your location, but here are some basics:

INSECT REPELLENT

ANTISEPTIC OINTMENT

SMALL SCISSORS

BAND-AIDS

BANDAGES

COMPASS

Compasses have been used for hundreds of years to point travelers in the right direction. Hold your compass flat and steady and it will always point north. Regularly check your compass to stay on track.

If you lose your compass, you can use the sun to give you basic directions. With some difference depending on the time of year, the sun rises in the east and sets in the west. In the northern hemisphere, the sun travels through the south to reach the west and in the southern hemisphere, through the north to reach the west. With this basic knowledge you can figure out roughly which way is north, east, south, and west.

TARPAULIN SHEET

This can be useful as **ground cover, rain protection,** or to make a **basic shelter.** (For a basic shelter you will also need a rope or a clothesline. See page 14.)

WATER PURIFICATION TABLETS

In emergencies, these can make fresh water drinkable. Choose tablets that **can be held without gloves.**

WHISTLE

Essential for **calling for help** or **alerting people** to your location.

ENERGY SUPPLY

Pack a bottle of water and cereal bars for an energy boost. Jelly beans are also useful for a quick energy rush. Think of them **as emergency equipment, not snacks!**

SLEEPING BAG

Your bag should be lightweight but provide the warmth you need. There are three basic shapes. Choose the one that's best for you.

TENT

Find a lightweight tent that's right for your climate. In a warm climate you may need no more than a hammock and a mosquito net, but in cold climates you will need a tent with insulated sides.

Easy to pitch. Best for short stays during good weather.

Very stable, but headroom is limited.

More headroom, but harder to put up.

Rectangular
This bag is roomy, but also quite heavy. Its shape is best suited to camping trips in warm conditions.

Mummy
This body-hugging, narrow bag retains the most heat and weighs less than the Rectangular. There is not much room to move inside, but it's great for survival in harsh conditions.

Semi-rectangular
This bag offers more room than the Mummy but is not as warm, and it's lighter and warmer than a Rectangular. It's the best pick if you're going backpacking.

BUILDING A CAMP

If you are going to be in one place for a while, you will need to build a camp, and if you don't have a tent, you will need to construct a shelter.

① PICK YOUR SITE

Follow these basic rules when deciding where to pitch camp:

Pick an area that is sheltered and **sloping slightly** so rainwater can drain away.

Make sure you are **near water.**

If you are in a national park, check if it has any **special rules** you need to follow.

Research the area and its wildlife. Avoid areas with berry bushes and other plants and fruits that attract animals, especially **bears.**

CHECK THE WEATHER

**Before you build your camp,
check the weather.**

If you don't know the weather forecast, the clouds can provide one!
As a rule, the higher, whiter, and fewer the clouds, the finer the weather.

Cumulus

*High, fluffy, white
scattered clouds*

FORECAST
Fair weather – but if they
join together, beware of
sudden showers.

Altostratus

*Gray, curtain-like clouds,
getting thicker and darker*

FORECAST
Rain is on its way!

Cirrus

Thick, wispy clouds

FORECAST
Fine, sunny weather,
perfect for camping.

Cumulonimbus

*Low, towering clouds,
appearing from near the
ground to up high*

FORECAST
Possibility of hail,
thunder, and lightning.

BUILD A BASIC SHELTER

If you don't have a tent, you will need shelter to give you shade or protect you from bad weather.

Tie a clothesline between two trees. Hang a tarpaulin sheet over the line and open it out to form a sloping roof. Weigh down the ends with stones. If you have enough tarpaulin, fold some under to make a dry floor. Before entering your shelter, make sure it is safe and sturdy.

CRITTER-PROOF YOUR CAMP

To avoid unwelcome visitors invading your camp, follow these top tips:

1 Keep all food **triple-wrapped** and as **far out of the reach of bears** and other animals as possible.

2 Store and eat your food **away from your shelter** – even tiny pieces of dropped food can attract unwanted nighttime visitors.

3 **Keep your camp clean.** The dirtier the camp, the more appealing it will be to bugs.

4 Set up a **toilet area away from your camp** and downstream from your water supply.

5 **Keep the lids on juice bottles:** the fruit attracts bugs.

SNAKES

! **Snakes curl around logs** and fallen tree branches, so if possible, choose a site on short grass or low-level plants.

! Stop snakes hiding in your kit by keeping as much of it **off the ground** as possible.

! Keep snakes out of your shelter by making sure it is **free of holes and gaps.** If you have a tent, keep it zipped up.

! **Never stick your hands into holes** without first checking what is inside.

! **Listen for rattlesnakes!** If you get too close, a rattlesnake will rattle its tail to warn you off.

If you see a snake ...

Snakes attack when they feel threatened, so **stay calm and back away slowly.**

. . . .

Never poke a snake with a stick, even if you think it is dead.

. . . .

If you are bitten, seek **immediate medical help** and describe what the snake looked like.

CAMP PLAN

Use this space to draw an ideal camp. Mark out:

lakes   rivers

water source   short grass

forests   beaches

ideal ground for your shelter

sloping areas   flat areas

secret hiding places for supplies

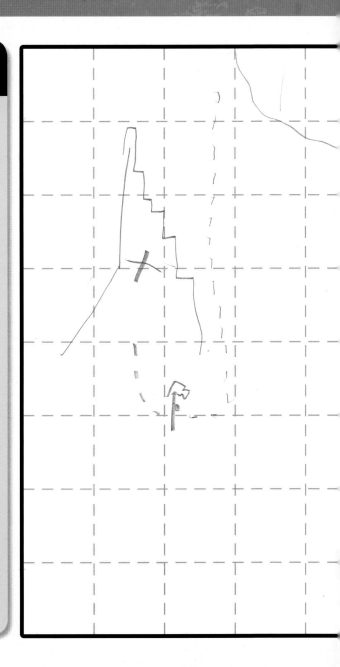

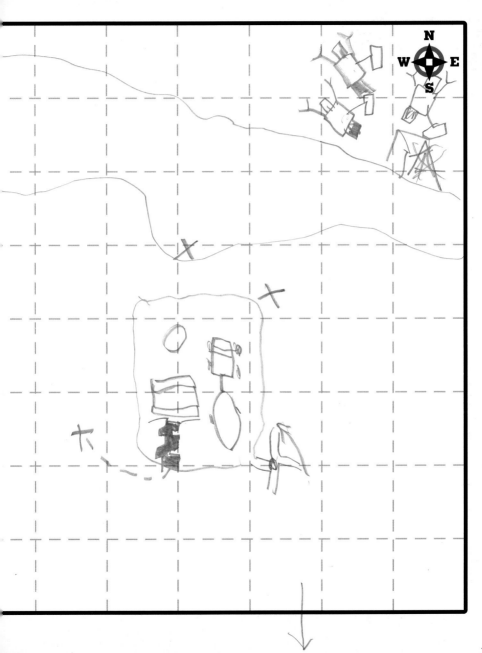

BASIC SURVIVAL SKILLS

Wherever you are, there are basic rules you can follow and skills you can learn to boost your chances of survival.

(1) ESSENTIAL KNOTS

Clove hitch

A clove hitch is a good way to tie a rope to a pole.
This could be essential when making a shelter.

1. Wrap the free end of a rope around a pole.

2. Cross the free end back over the rope and the pole, then slip the free end underneath the last wrap.

3. Pull the free end tightly to secure the knot.

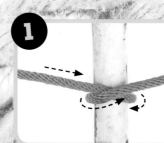

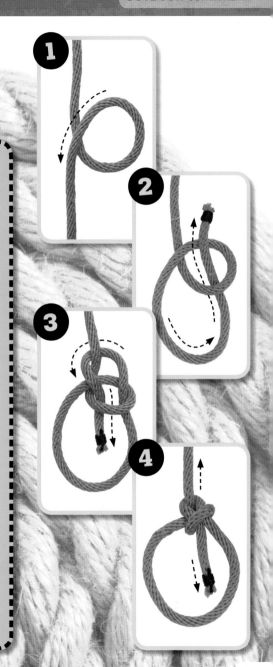

Bowline

The bowline knot creates a fixed loop that is firm but also easy to untie.
The loop can be big enough to lift someone from danger or small enough to hang food supplies from a branch, out of the reach of bears.

1. Cross the ends of your rope to make the size of loop you need.

2. Following the arrows on the diagram, make a small loop over the rope, then thread the free end up through the main loop from the underside.

3. Take the free end around the long end of the rope and bring it back through the small loop.

4. Pull the ends of the rope to tighten the knot. The loop should stay firm and stable yet remain easy to untie.

(2) FOOD AND WATER

Water is your most vital resource. It is possible to survive three weeks without food, but only three days without water. If you run out of food or water, follow these steps for obtaining emergency supplies.

1 **Water always runs downhill,** so look in valleys for streams and pools.

WARNING!

A pool that has no plants growing around it **may be polluted.**

2 **You can collect water from a plant** by tying a plastic bag around its leaves. Water that would evaporate into the air will be caught in the bag.

3 Once you have collected water from a stream or pool, **make it safe to drink with your purification tablets** (see page 10).

4 Emergency food supplies should be **lightweight and small,** like trail mix. The more you eat, the thirstier you will be, so eat just enough to keep you going.

WARNING!

Do not eat something unless you know it is **100% safe.**

20

CALLING FOR HELP

If you are stranded or lost and have no phone signal, there are still ways you can send out an emergency message.

Morse code is a language made from dashes and dots. Use your flashlight to send out an SOS, the international signal for help:

1 three quick flashes
(dot dot dot)

2 three slow flashes
(dash dash dash)

3 three quick flashes
(dot dot dot)

International rescue

Think of five countries you'd like to visit, then research the words "help me" in their languages and write this in the grid.

Country (language)	Words for "help me"
France (French)	*M'Aidez!*

Be seen and heard

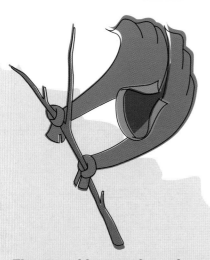

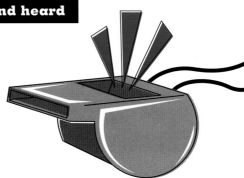

Blow your whistle
if you think help is near.

Tie your shirt to a branch and wave it like a flag when you see a car, boat, or helicopter approaching. If you cannot make a flag, wave your arms.

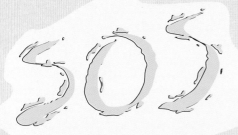

Write SOS in the sand using a stick, or with stones in a forest clearing. The letters should be as large as possible.

ARE YOU LOST?

If you are lost but in a safe place, assess whether it would be better to stay where you are and conserve your energy and supplies or continue searching for help. **Staying in one place may make you easier to find.**

Secrets of Extreme Survival

SNOWBOUND SURVIVAL

Snow, ice, and freezing cold temperatures affect most of the world at some point in the year, so be prepared to survive the chill!

BUILD A SNOW FORT

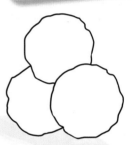

1 Fort building is cold work, so **equip yourself** with warm, waterproof gloves, snow boots, and extra layers of clothing.

2 **Check the snow.** If the snow is powdery and you cannot make a snowball, it will not stick together to make your fort's walls.

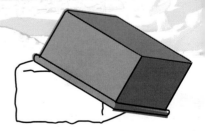

3 Use a stick to **mark out the border** of your fort in the snow. Remember that you will need an entrance!

4 **Make bricks using a bucket.** Pack snow into the bucket, then turn it out like a sand castle.

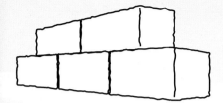

5 **Build your walls** around the marked border. Copy the pattern of brick walls and fill the gaps with handfuls of snow. Make sure the walls are going straight up and down, not leaning at different angles. The walls should be high enough for you to comfortably crouch behind.

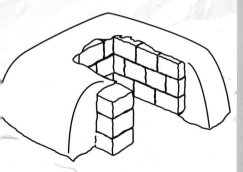

6 To strengthen the walls, **pack extra snow around the fort.** Smooth the sides so they slant slightly, like the sides of a pyramid leaning into each other.

ARCTIC SURVIVAL
TOP TIPS

! **Wear at least four layers** of light, warm clothing, such as fleece pullovers or jackets.

• •

! Wear a **thermal hat, boots, and gloves.** In freezing conditions, up to 40% of your body heat can be lost through your head.

• •

! **Stay on white ground.** Brown or gray ground is likely to be unsafe ice and may not carry your weight.

• •

! **Keep well-fuelled** with energy-boosting food, such as nuts, cereal bars, and bananas.

• •

! **Carry special flares** to scare off polar bears.

DESERT SURVIVAL

Everyone knows that deserts get hot – as high as 122°F (50°C) – but at night the temperature can drop to 32°F (0°C), so you need to be prepared to keep warm as well as cool.

BUILD A SHELTER BELOW GROUND

WARNING!

Building anything in the desert is sweaty work. **Always work during the cooler periods.**

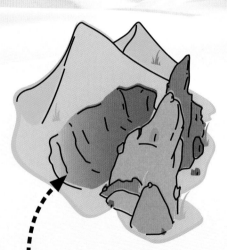

1 **Pick a spot** between sand dunes or rocks and **dig a trench** that's long enough and wide enough for you to lie in – but **look out for snakes and scorpions.**

2 Use the sand you dig up to **make a low wall** around the two long sides and one of the short sides.

3 The side without a wall is your entrance. Dig down deeper at this point to make it easier to get in and out.

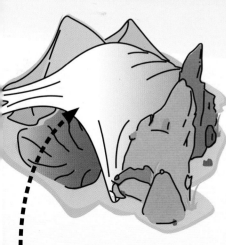

4 Cover the trench with a canvas sheet and secure it with rocks.

DESERT SURVIVAL
TOP TIPS

! **Keep as covered-up as possible** to minimize sunburn and stop water evaporating from your body. Light clothing reflects heat away from your body, but dark clothing gives better UV protection.

! **Always be on the lookout for shade.** If you don't have anything else, large rocks and cacti give shelter from the sun.

! **Walk and work during the night** when it is cooler, then sleep and rest during the day.

! When searching for water, **look for animal footprints.** They will often lead to a supply.

TORNADOES

Tornadoes are deadly winds that can strike with very little warning, so planning ahead is key to survival.

IF YOU ARE
INDOORS

! **Plan in advance where your shelter will be.** This must be away from windows and preferably underground, so a basement is ideal. If you don't have a basement, ground-level cupboards can also make good shelters. When the tornado is approaching, **keep low and cover your head.**

! **Keep an emergency supply** of food, water, spare clothes, liquid soap, a first-aid kit, a flashlight, and a whistle to let people know where you are. Having a battery-operated or wind-up radio will allow you to keep up with announcements from the emergency services.

IF YOU ARE
OUTDOORS

! **Find a shelter as quickly as possible.** If you are in a car, get out and find a shelter.

! If you can't find a shelter, **lie down in a ditch** and cover your head and neck.

EARTHQUAKES

Earthquakes are caused by movements of rock within the earth, which make the land above shake and split.

IF YOU ARE INDOORS

! **Designate safe areas in your home.** For example, under furniture or against an inside wall that is well away from **windows or objects that could fall on you.**

! **Keep emergency supplies** (see *Tornadoes*) in an easy-to-reach place.

! At the first sign of a quake, remember: **Drop, Cover, and Hold,** or cover your head and neck with your arms and don't move!

! **Stay where you are until the shaking stops.** Don't move until you know it is safe or someone has instructed you to move.

! **Listen to your battery-operated radio** for instructions and news.

WARNING!

Earthquakes may last for less than a minute, but they are often followed by mini earthquakes called aftershocks.

IF YOU ARE OUTDOORS

! **Find a spot clear of anything that could fall on you,** such as trees and posts, and **lie on the ground.**

! If you are in a car, **the driver should pull off the road** and stay parked until the shaking stops.

VOLCANOES

When volcanoes erupt, fast-flowing rivers of lava, ash, mud, rocks, and water can cause devastating damage.

! Scientists monitor volcanoes consistently and should be able to give warning of an eruption. **Always follow the advice of the authorities.**

! Lava can flow at speeds of 40 mph (65 km/h). It can cause water levels to rise, resulting in floods. If there is a risk of flooding, **move to higher ground.**

! Be prepared with **goggles** and **long-sleeved tops** and **pants** to protect you from ash fall. Holding a damp cloth over your face will help you breathe.

CLASSIFIED

LIGHTNING

Lightning bolts during storms are caused by electric charges within clouds. Being struck by lightning is extremely dangerous.

IF YOU ARE INDOORS

Unplug electrical items, and **do not lean against walls** as they may contain wires that could carry the lightning's electricity. For the same reason, do not use phones with cords or touch pipes and taps.

IF YOU ARE OUTDOORS

! **Never take shelter by tall trees** as they may be hit and knocked down by the lightning.

! **Keep clear of water** as it conducts electricity and is dangerous if struck by lightning.

! **Stay away from any metal items** as they can carry electricity. Don't forget that this includes everyday items like umbrellas, which have metal parts, and keys.

Lightning produces thunderclaps. The claps take a few seconds to be heard because sound travels more slowly than light.

You can tell how far away a storm is by counting the seconds between the lightning and the thunder. The storm will be around 1 mi (1.5 km) away for every five seconds you count.

HEAT WAVES

A heat wave takes place when the highest daily temperature for five days is 9°F (5°C) higher than normal.

 Close blinds and shades to keep rooms cool.

 Cancel outdoor sports and activities.

 Never leave pets in a car: It will be far too hot for them.

 Drink plenty of water and avoid fizzy drinks containing caffeine as this will dehydrate you.

 Avoid wearing tight-fitting, dark clothes as these will suck in the heat.

 If you don't have air-conditioning, think of **cool places** you can go, such as shopping centers and the library. But **avoid moving too quickly from the extreme heat to the cold:** it won't make you feel good and can be dangerous.

BEARS

Bears love food! And thanks to their strong sense of smell, they can sniff out a dead animal from up to 20 mi (32 km) away.

If you see a bear before it sees you, **back away slowly.** But if the bear sees you first, **start talking calmly.** Once the bear hears that you are human, it is likely to walk away.

If the bear appears aggressive, **try to remain calm** and don't run (it can move faster than you). **Back away slowly, but don't make eye contact.**

PIRANHAS

Sharp-toothed piranhas live in the warm waters of South America. Though they are more likely to attack other fish than humans, they are best avoided.

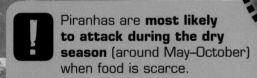

! Piranhas are **most likely to attack during the dry season** (around May–October) when food is scarce.

! **Don't enter water with an open cut,** as the blood will attract the fish.

! If you have touched raw meat, **wash your hands before entering the water** because the fish will sense a snack on your hands.

! If warning signs say **don't go in the water, don't!**

KEEP OUT OF THE WATER!

SWARMING BEES

A swarm of bees may look terrifying, but since stinging things kills them, using their stings is a last resort.

A swarm appears when a hive becomes **overcrowded** and thousands of bees journey to find a new home.

If you see a swarm heading in your direction, **get out of the way and take cover** – indoors, if possible.

If you can't go indoors, make sure you **cover your face and eyes.**

WARNING!

Once **one bee stings,** the other bees will join in.

! **Don't hide underwater:** bees can hover over a lake longer than you can hold your breath.

! **Keep calm! Never hit bees** or attempt to brush them away: This will only annoy them and make them more likely to sting.

! If you do get stung, it's important to **remove the stinger quickly,** so find help immediately.

CROCODILES

! Crocodiles can **swim at up to 25 mph (40 km/h**

Crocodiles have a deadly bite, stronger than any other known creature. There are 23 species of crocodiles and their relatives, and some are more aggressive than others. Research your area to assess the danger level.

! As a basic rule, **obey danger signs** and stay out of the water if you are in an area inhabited by crocodiles. If you fall into crocodile-infested waters, **swim to shore as quietly and calmly as you can**. Splashing and yelling can attract crocodiles and make them attack.

! If you are setting up camp by the water, **take local advice on how far away you should pitch your tent** from the water's edge.

! In extreme situations, people have **saved themselves** from a crocodile attack by **hitting the croc's eyes and nose.**

! On land, crocodiles can **run at up to 10 mph (17 km/h)** but will tire quickly. If you are chased by a crocodile, run as fast as you can **AWAY from the water.**

! Find out if it is **mating season**. During this period **female crocodiles will be particularly fierce** and protect their eggs with force.

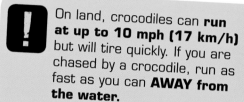

CROCODILE OR ALLIGATOR: WHAT'S THE DIFFERENCE?

! Though both should be avoided, generally **alligators are less aggressive than crocodiles.**

! As a rule, an **alligator has a U-shaped snout while a crocodile has a V-shaped snout.**

! In addition, **crocodiles show all their teeth when their mouths are closed,** whereas alligators only show their top row.

WARNING!

Floating crocs look like logs!

Crocodile

Alligator

ELEPHANTS

A "mock charge" means the elephant has no real intention of going after you. However, it's best not to take risks, so plan to follow these rules:

If you're confronted by an elephant, try to determine whether it's preparing to chase you or is assessing how dangerous you are by performing a "mock charge."

The following signs could indicate a "mock charge":

Twitching **trunk**
Relaxed or fanned **ears**
Swinging a **leg**

! **Do not turn your back** on the elephant and run. This will only encourage it to chase you.

! **If you must run, move in a zigzag.** This may confuse the elephant, but also make you harder to chase – it's difficult for an elephant to change direction because of its weight. But **beware:** An elephant can run at up to **25 mph (40 km/h).**

! **Try to stay downwind** from the elephant to prevent it from following your scent.

! **Find a shield,** such as a rock, or climb a tree – but be confident it's not one the elephant can knock down!

! **Don't jump into water.** Elephants are strong swimmers.

! **Wave your arms and yell.** If all else fails, this may scare the elephant away.

Create Your Own

Secret Survival Plans

SECRET SURVIVAL PLANS

Survival plans are essential for facing extreme conditions, but they can also help you with everyday events.

Here are some of the times you may need a survival plan:

if you're grounded

a bike ride

when visiting relatives

any time boredom strikes

a long car journey

a family vacation

a visit to the mall with your parents

if a storm is forecast

a camping trip

when you're looking after your kid brother or sister

SECRET SURVIVAL PLAN

Situation

	High	Medium	Low
Danger level			
Top-secret level			

Equipment and clothing

SECRET SURVIVAL PLAN

Situation

	High	Medium	Low
Danger level			
Top-secret level			

Equipment and clothing

Do

Don't

At the back of the book, you will find survival planning documents to cut out and seal with a sticker. Think about what equipment you will need, how dangerous or secret the situation is, and the things you must remember to do or not do. Use what you've learned in this book and research further online or at your local library.

SURVIVAL KITS

Having special storage for your equipment and plans is essential to survival success. The size and type of storage will depend on your situation. There are four types of secret survival kits.

SECRET SURVIVAL STORAGE KIT (SSSK)

A **large capacity kit** designed to be hidden in your room – most likely **under your bed.** You can have more than one of these hidden in different places.

Shoe boxes or large cereal boxes make ideal SSSKs. Keep them protected with a special knot or **seal them with tape or a sticker.**

Placing a small, lightweight item, such as a cornflake, in a special place on top of the box will let you know if your box has been **moved by prying parents, brothers, sisters, or friends.**

PORTABLE SECRET SURVIVAL KIT (PSSK

Designed for **on-the-move survival,** PSSKs are **smaller than SSSKs** and can easily be carried in backpacks.

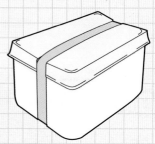

Square tubs with snap-on lids (often used for spreads or ice cream) make good PSSKs. Make sure the tub is clean and **use a large elastic band or tape to keep the lid secure.**

Label your kit with a **Top Secret** sticker.

ULTRA-SECRET SURVIVAL KIT (USSK)

Best for **smaller super-secret items** that need to be hidden in plain sight, **such as message decoders or emergency provisions.**

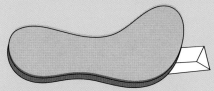

Thick old unwanted books make great USSKs. Cut a neat rectangle on the tenth page, then use the hole as a template to draw and cut out more rectangles. Stop when the hole is deep enough for your kit.

For flat items, such as messages, plans, or codes, you can turn an **old sneaker or shoe into a secret hiding place** by creating a false insole. Either buy a custom-made insole or create your own. Draw around your shoe on stiff cardboard. Cut around the shape, making sure that it will fit neatly inside your shoe. Place your plans or messages inside the shoe and cover them with your false insole.

WARNING!

Be careful when using scissors!

SLIMLINE MINI SURVIVAL KIT (SMSK)

Designed to be **carried in a pocket and kept close to you wherever you are,** indoors or out.

Old CD cases, wallets, and candy boxes make great storage for small items of equipment, such as Band-Aids, string, gum, a compass, or a pen. Label your kit with a sticker.

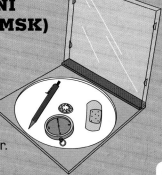

CODES AND CIPHERS

There are times when switching to a secret language is the only way to ensure your security in a survival situation.

CODES

A code is a word, phrase, symbol, or action that has a special secret meaning. For example, "What's on TV tonight?" could be code for "Let's scram!" **Here are some more examples:**

Coughing code

This is an easy way to pass on a message without anyone knowing what you are doing. It's especially good at a party, dinner table, or family gathering. First, agree on up to **three messages you may wish to pass on to your accomplice** (any more and there's a good chance you'll be discovered). For example, at a party, one cough might mean: "I'm hungry, let's find a snack!"; two coughs: "I'm bored, let's watch some TV!"; and three: "I'm tired let's go home!"

Devise a coughing code here:

Number of coughs	Meaning

Object placement

This is a super-sneaky way to communicate agreed-upon messages without anyone else having a clue what you are saying. For example, if you are at a family event, you might agree with your brother or sister that **if things get really dull and you want to leave the room, you will place an empty cup on the windowsill.** Or you can agree that if you leave a certain book open over the arm of a chair, it means that food supplies are hidden under the sofa!

Face codes

Face codes work a bit like object placement. Simply agree on messages that will be communicated by touching different parts of your face. So touching your nose might mean "Let's go!" or touching your chin might mean "Let's stay!" **Face codes are great when you are in crowded spaces or at different ends of a room.**

Devise a face code here:

Face code	Meaning

CIPHERS

A cipher is a form of secret message writing. To create a simple cipher, first write the alphabet and then write an alternative letter, symbol, or number (or a combination of all three) below it. Using this cipher, the word "survival" becomes "dgwayaiq."

A	B	C	D	E	F	G	H	I	J	K	L	M	N	O	P	Q	R	S	T	U	V	W	X	Y	Z
I	F	L	R	C	T	V	N	Y	B	M	Q	E	H	X	Z	K	W	D	P	G	A	U	O	S	J

Devise your own ciphers here:

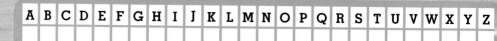

A	B	C	D	E	F	G	H	I	J	K	L	M	N	O	P	Q	R	S	T	U	V	W	X	Y	Z

A	B	C	D	E	F	G	H	I	J	K	L	M	N	O	P	Q	R	S	T	U	V	W	X	Y	Z

A	B	C	D	E	F	G	H	I	J	K	L	M	N	O	P	Q	R	S	T	U	V	W	X	Y	Z

Now write a secret message:

PARENT-PROOFING YOUR ROOM

If you can't lock your room or drawers, there are easy parent-proofing measures you can take to keep your plans and equipment secret.

(1) FALSE DRAWER

1 **Empty your sock drawer and measure** its inside length and width.

2 **Cut a stiff piece of cardboard** just slightly smaller than the drawer, so it fits neatly inside.

3 **Place your secret documents or equipment in the drawer**, then find four objects of a similar height to act as posts – **they must be taller than whatever you have hidden.**

4 **Arrange the objects in the drawer, then put the card over the top** to create a false bottom. Pile your socks or underwear on top.

5 **Your secrets will be concealed** even if someone looks in the drawer.

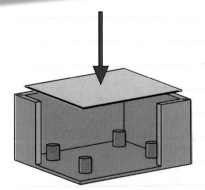

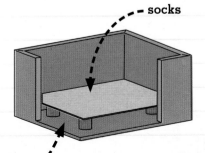

socks

secret stuff

47

TOP SECRET

2

FAKE BOOKSHELF

1 **Hide large items behind a fake row of books.**
First, find a box that will be big enough to hold your items, but small enough to sit on a shelf in your room.

2 **Use spines from the dustjackets of unwanted hardback books** to cover the front of the box. Source your books from yard sales and thrift stores. **NEVER** use a book from your home without getting permission first.

3 **Cut off the front and back covers** – leaving the spine and enough to fold in – and press down to create a neat edge.

4 Next, **tape the spines together in a row** and stick them on the front of your box so they look like a row of books. Put real books on either side of your box.

MORE TOP HIDING PLACES

Under your **mattress**

· ·

Inside empty **battery compartments** of electronics

· ·

In a zip-up **cushion**

· ·

Behind **posters** or pictures

· ·

Inside old **shoes** at the back of a closet

CLASSIFIED

SNOOPER TRAPS

Setting simple traps will let you know if someone has been looking through your things.

Cotton traps

Leave a small length of cotton on the floor either just inside your door or around ultra-secret areas of your room. If anyone walks over the cotton, it should move, and you will know you've had intruders!

Take a picture

Take photos or draw pictures of the high-security areas of your room. If anything gets moved, you'll soon know!

Hair trap

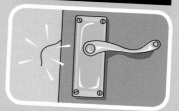

1. **Pull a single hair from your head**, then tape it low down on the outside of a door frame.

2. As you close the door, **push the hair in so it is bent round at a right angle.**

3. **If the door is opened while you are out, the hair will ping out.** You can also use this snooper trap to secure boxes and drawers.

SECRET DOTS

Place small hole-punch dots in secret places on or around high-security items. Keep an accurate note or take a picture of where you put them. **If they are moved, you'll know your things have been tampered with.**

PLAN YOUR ROOM

Use this space to map out your room. Include the secret hiding places and high-security areas requiring snooper traps.

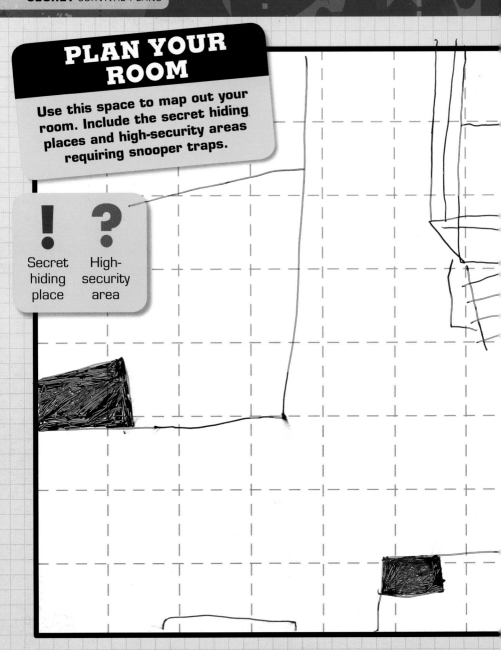

!
Secret hiding place

?
High-security area

SECRET SURVIVAL FILE

Make a secret file to keep your plans safe.

1. Cut along the line marked (A).

2. Next, turn the page and put the two pages together by taping along the side and bottom.

A

Secret Survival Plans

SECRET SURVIVAL PLAN

Situation use our powers
Ella and Me

	High	Medium	Low
Danger level	☐	☐	☐
Top-secret level	☑	☐	☐

Equipment and clothing Non

Do use our powers

Don't Let eny one know

SECRET SURVIVAL PLAN

Situation

	High	Medium	Low
Danger level	☐	☐	☐
Top-secret level	☐	☐	☐

Equipment and clothing

Do

Don't

SECRET SURVIVAL PLAN

Situation

Danger level

Top-secret level

High   Medium   Low

Equipment and clothing

Do

Don't

SECRET SURVIVAL PLAN

Situation

Danger level

Top-secret level

High   Medium   Low

Equipment and clothing

Do

Don't

SECRET SURVIVAL PLAN

Situation

Danger level

Top-secret level

High Medium Low

Equipment and clothing

Do

Don't

SECRET SURVIVAL PLAN

Situation

Danger level

Top-secret level

High Medium Low

Equipment and clothing

Do

Don't